From your Spirit Brother…

Introduction

This book was written and inspired after my forty days of fasting last year (2019), when each of my 24-hour cycle revealed to me keys that would help me unlock my ***true nature***.

Present day humanity is so lost in the accumulative stresses and pressures of life, carrying all forms of mental and emotional baggage, bodily tension and all sorts of fears, be it fear of rejection or of pain, guilt or even shame. As energetic beings that we are, these negative experiences, over time, become energy that get stuck in our bodies, forming habits, and the cycles of our actions and thinking becomes a perpetual wheel that is followed by pain and more suffering.

The aim of this book is to offer you pearls of wisdom that will help you find your way back home, to ***who you really are***! Each petal aims to light your path and guide you to where you need to go so you don't get lost again, and I hope that as you read and contemplate on each page, the lessons will become real and start to be experienced by you in your every day and may all your daily cares and concerns drop off naturally as your ***true nature*** is revealed by the light of your ***true awareness***.

40 Petals for Daily Contemplations

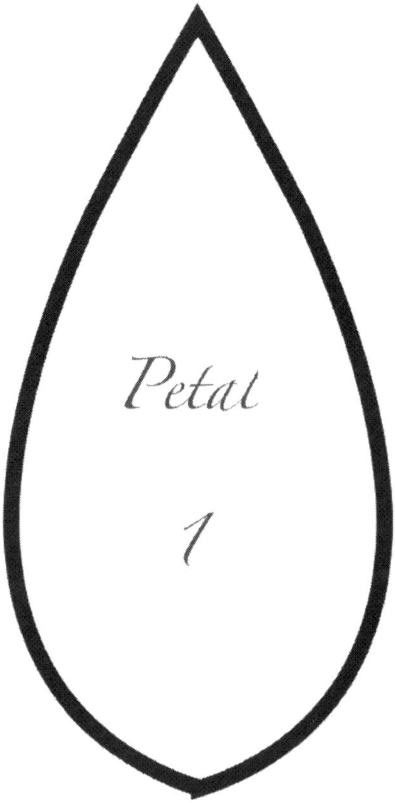
Petal
1

Petal 1

The ***mind*** abides in a state of still, flowing water, gripping and holding on to nothing, allowing the currents to move from one to the next without any direction or destination to get to. It moves as it wills.

The ***heart*** always open, positioned in a place where it can speak to you and whisper clear insights and always ready to love, forgive and let go.

The ***gut*** discerning clearly - that which is a 'yes' being a 'yes!' and a 'no' being a 'no!', clearly discerning that which needs to be separated, and thus, bringing you to a place where there is ***zero*** confusion.

Lesson

Allow the three to move freely to become one.

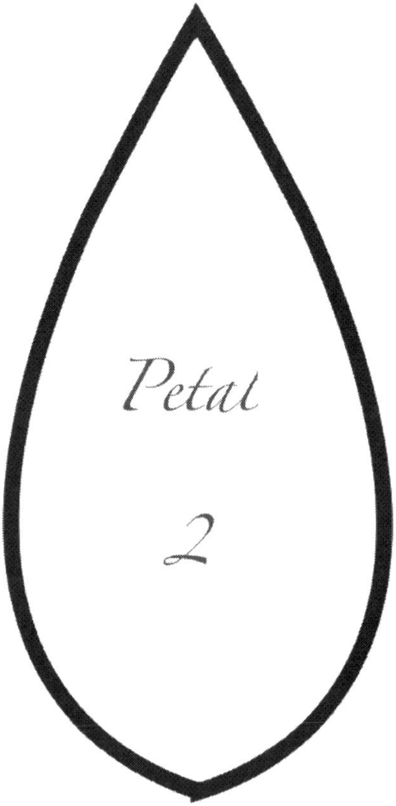
Petal
2

Petal 2

Care nothing about what others may think or say about you. For the 'you' that they are referring to is in fact, not you! But rather, their own thoughts and projection, working through the lens of their own 'self'. A 'self' with distorted views of reality, otherwise, there would be no judgment but just a ***mirror*** watching.

Lesson

Free yourself from the care of what others might think or say, knowing that there is no difference between their views and the wind blowing.

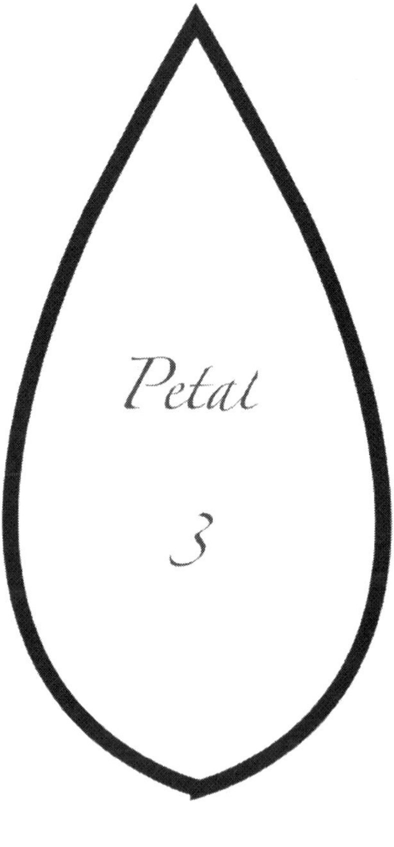
Petal
3

Petal 3

Unless one can sit in full acceptance of how life has become, that which needs to rise and drop will only cling. Full, whole-hearted acceptance, is required in each and every moment of one's life, creating an atmosphere for all to rise and all to drop. This is the key to being free from the grip of one's past and the demands of one's future. It's simple, ***full acceptance***.

Lesson

Allow all to rise and all to fall.

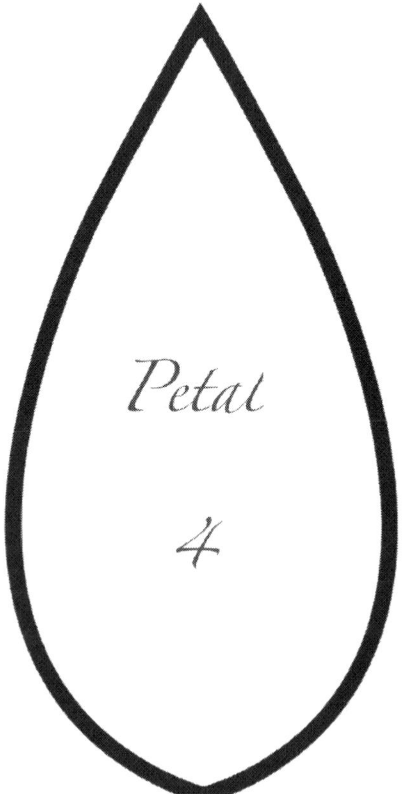
Petal
4

Petal 4

There is nowhere to get to, for you are everything that you are seeking. You are the outcome, the finished prize, completed and whole. So ***trust*** that which is walking, that which is travelling and that which is journeying. For everything you are is already complete in this very moment.

Lesson

You are that which you seek.

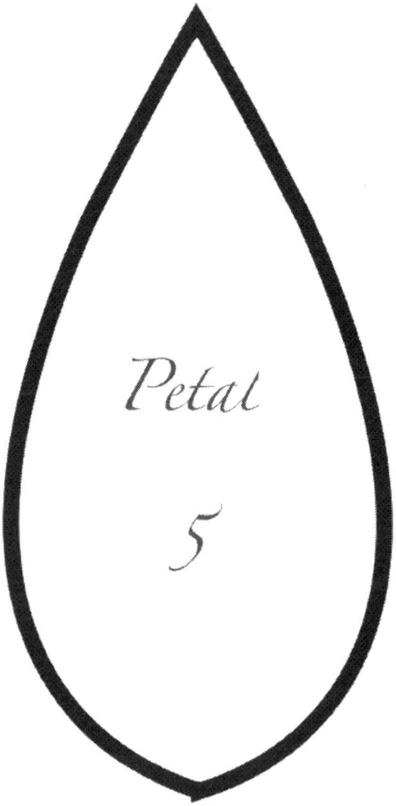
Petal
5

Petal 5

To live life fully is to know that one can only live life like this, in and through the gateway of ***awareness***. Thoughts and thinking are not the same mechanism as awareness. For you to experience life in its entirety, all of your inner vehicles must surrender and join that which is present; your true light of awareness and your very presence. And then this is only half the journey. The second half, once you are living through the gateway of awareness, is to marry all your actions without any hesitation. While you're walking, walk. While you're eating, eat. While you're working, work – All pointing to the ONE.

Lesson

Combine your vehicles together and live through them whole-heartedly.

Petal
6

Petal 6

Everything has a speed, a tempo and a rhythm. Some move quicker than others. Cars move quicker than motorbikes, motorbikes move quicker than birds, and airplanes move quicker than all of them. However, none should influence your internal harmony and rhythm. Once you know that there is nowhere to get to, nowhere to climb, nowhere to be late to, your roots settle like a tree deeply rooted in the soil of eternity, allowing life to ***flow*** through you, allowing space and time to pass, allowing clouds to change, yet your presence mirrors a mountain, immovable and steadfast.

Lesson

Never be in a rush to get anywhere for there is nowhere to get to.

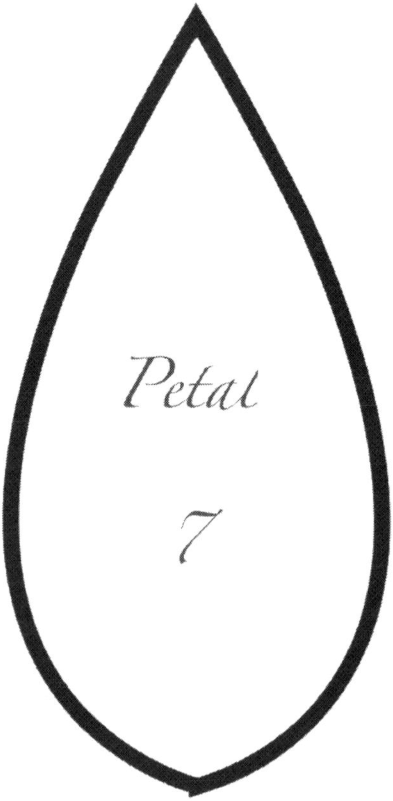
Petal
7

Petal 7

As we observe the breath, there is an inhalation and exhalation. So there is an inner awareness and an outer action that always marries the awareness. Always trust the cycles of your 24-hours to provide you with the right action, enabling you to pass through every opportunity to ***liberate*** yourself from suffering. When the light of your awareness is revealed and whispers a word of wisdom, do not hesitate to walk it through. Simply join with the action and become one with it.

Lesson

To complete the circle, or to complete any cycle, one has to marry action with insight, or insight with action.

Petal
8

Petal 8

At all times remember that you are always enough, meaning that you are fully complete and whole as you are. You are the beginning and the end, in this very moment. You are the prize, in and of itself. This way, you will never leave your True Self. Searching for another one, journeying to far destinations only to find that all that is living is pointing to you, here and now. There are no mistakes and in this, there is no room for wavering or doubt. ***You are enough***, you've always been enough and you will always be enough.

Lesson

Settle in the knowing that you are enough.

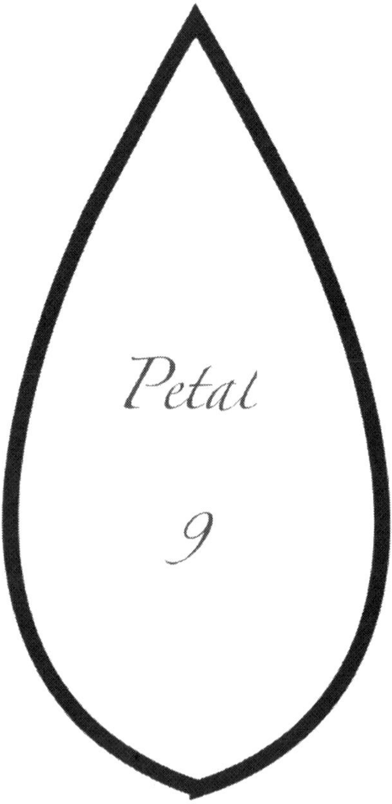
Petal
9

Petal 9

Every action should be treated with the same respect, with the same level of awareness and concentration because there is no high or low, good or bad, up or down. There is only action, reality or life. All action offers you the same opportunity for you to ***merge*** with it. But there is an action that is liberating and there is action that is binding. For this reason, awareness should always come first. Allowing the inner whisper, the inner light of your awareness to reveal and unfold your path. The Way will always give you shadows and signposts as to which way you should walk. But let me remind you of the Law of Circles. If you don't take action and you hesitate instead, these circles will reappear. This is the Law of Karma - the Law of Cause and Effect.

Lesson

Be quick to act when wisdom speaks.

Petal
10

Petal 10

Allowing things to rise and things to fall is also allowing yourself the opportunity to walk through the gates of your fears. Unless you are willing to pass and confront your fears, your practice is only half complete. For sitting and walking have to merge and become one. The female opens the gate, and the male walks through. This is the true meaning of passing and walking through life fully, whole-heartedly, full action with an inner courage and a determination and motivation to liberate always. In liberation, I mean, giving your true self an opportunity to know and experience one's self. This is your highest calling, your ***true purpose***, the real reason you are here. Waste no time.

Lesson

Understanding your true calling is to experience one's self, but to experience one's self you must allow room for the true Self to be experienced. It is not enough just to sit.

Petal
11

Petal 11

Non-clinging or non-holding is essential in allowing life to reveal Life, for clinging and holding are mere distortions and fears holding the true Self back from flowing because when we cling or hold on to what we think is right or wrong we are merely creating ripples of karmic tension. And when tension arises energy gets misdirected. However, 'non- holding' and 'non-gripping' is allowing life to flow as it should, in the moment. This is called ***It Breathes You***. For this, you are not required.

Lesson

Remember not to cling or hold, for It Breathes You!

Petal
12

Petal 12

Sitting like a mirror, reflecting life as it is without any distortion is very different to 'refracting' light. For when one refracts light it changes its position and angle, and so the light bounces off and creates a distortion of the same light. Sit therefore with your true authentic Self. This is the real meaning of sitting in your true Self, allowing life to be in the Presence through your presence. This is the true meaning of ***sitting like a mirror***.

Lesson

See things as they are with no judgments or internal motives.

Petal
13

Petal 13

There is always a ***female and a male*** in everything – a contraction and expansion, a listening and a speaking, a sitting and a walking, but the female always comes first otherwise focus will lose its awareness. Concentration will lose its attention. Concentration, focus, speech, intention are always serving the awareness. Otherwise things become too one-sided, too intense and then eventually break.

Lesson

The female (awareness) always comes first. So, always be in awareness in all your doing and with all your being.

Petal
14

Petal 14

All things in Nature are always pointing towards Life always working together in this great project we call Life, very much like your heart, lungs, kidneys and liver, separate in their function yet they are married and focused in this one sustaining factor. They are all working towards Life. This is the Law of One-ness. It is everywhere. The wind blows the seed, the seeds drops and the earth catches it. The soil opens, the seed enters and begins its sacred journey, slowing yielding to the natural life currents that are all working together. So 'trust and let go' is in the ***knowing*** that life, in itself, is doing the work. Just as the seed trusted the wind and the soil, so you too must trust the invisible currents. It is breathing you!

Lesson

Learn to trust Life.

Petal
15

Petal 15

You have all been given life – air to breathe, a sun that shines, food to eat, trees that provide you with shade, oxygen and water to drink. In every direction you gaze life is giving you life. Even when you gaze upwards and see the clouds that give us water or even further towards the sun that gives life to all things. Everywhere you turn to life is giving you life. Therefor knowing this, knowing that the trees gently and lovingly provide you with this gesture of love, and the sweetness of their fruit, have you ever stopped to give thanks? Have you ever stopped to bow and acknowledge them? This is the real meaning of ***gratitude***.

Lesson

Give thanks.

Petal
16

Petal 16

Your true nature is all that Nature is. The sun, the moon, the stars, the trees have all one thing in common – ***authentic and whole***, complete, enough - all reflecting your true Self. So sitting in this vast mirror and reflection of 'enough-ness' is also acknowledging your enough-ness. When you sit in front of a tree and it sits in front of you, you are in fact looking at yourself. This is the true meaning of sitting like a mirror. But only those with eyes to see, and ears to hear, will capture the beauty of this essence.

Lesson

We are all mirrors, all reflecting one.

Petal
17

Petal 17

The way of the moment can only be felt and experienced if the shoes you are wearing are journeying ***one step at a time***. For there is no moving forward or backward. There is only change and life moving much like a leaf floating and moving in a river, gently moving from one place to the next, and yet, resting calmly on the waters and currents of life.

Lesson

Take one moment at a time.

Petal
18

Petal 18

If the mind thinks 'like or dislike', 'in or out', 'love or hate', 'good or bad', then you have entered the realm of delusion and judgment. For there is never two, but only ***that which is existing.*** The Law of Cause and Effect, and it's soon passing. Thoughts that are thinking are just thoughts trying to understand this law or grasp the moment, creating views and opinions or further judgments, creating further ideas and constructs and restricting nature to flow and reveal what it truly is. All this must be allowed to pass through without grasping or holding onto. That which needs to speak will speak.

Lesson

Listening and thinking are not the same.

Petal
19

Petal 19

There is no standpoint or foundation other than you are always enough, AS YOU ARE. This is the foundational law of all. For all is working as it should be, as it's meant to be. Allowing yourself to experience this enough-ness settles you entirely into the moment. This is the key to experiencing your true presence and this is your birthright. In fact, it is your reality. For there is no "I" that needs to be complete or has to be completed. ***You are IT***, in this moment. So if one allows one's self to sink into this reality, then the full reality that is all around will remind one daily.

Lesson

Sink into the reality that you are enough.

Petal
20

Petal 20

Your true light, life and essence, disappears before your very eyes when you grab on to the idea, concept or belief, that you exist separately from the All. However, the moment you remember that life is living through you and for you and that you were never required in this magical process, then Oneness appears again. This is the true meaning of ***'you are not required'***. You are not required is only a reminder for your false self to stop interfering with the eternal flow that is always here and now.

Lesson

You are not required.

Petal
21

Petal 21

Many have come and have said, "I am the Way, the Truth and the Life" but in fact You are the Way, the Truth and the Life, the Path, the Journey, the Presence, the Joy, the Peace. Everything life is, you are also. So why practice if you already are? Real practice is a reminder to one's self to ***not interfere*** with this reality. Seeing yourself as part of the All is to move and breathe as you should.

Lesson

Seeing your true Self clearly.

Petal
22

Petal 22

You may ask "What is the most conducive atmospheric conditions for me to experience my essence?" The Here and the Now, or the Now and the Here, are just words to describe the atmosphere of non-interference. This happens by itself, through itself, when we embrace stillness openly without judgment and allow all things to be. The moment we do this we enter into the practice of ***Meditation***. This is why meditation is essential.

Lesson

Meditate daily.

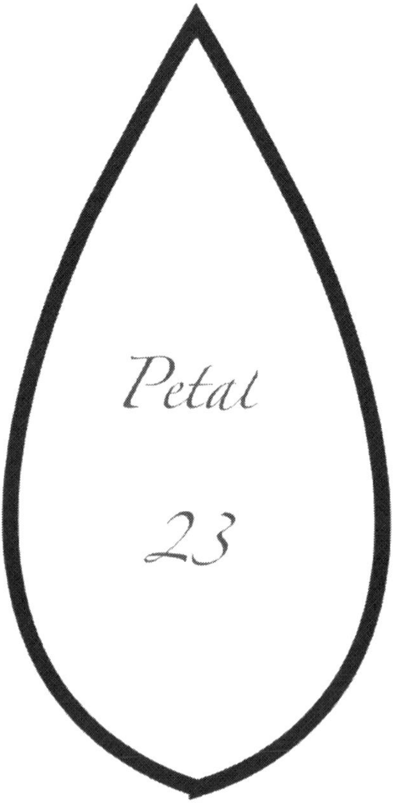
Petal
23

Petal 23

Being entirely present means there is no separation between yourself and ‘things’, or yourself and the ‘action’ of things. If separation exists between you and the action or the object then you are giving energy space to move and create, to have a pause, and thus an effect. Very much like how traffic accumulates. Eventually it moves in all directions, creating further noise and toxicity, which can materialize blind spots and can cause a crash. And the crash is a reminder to listen, sit, rest and ***return home***.

Lesson

Be mindful not to habitually create a separation between you and an object and you and your action.

Petal
24

Petal 24

The false self, or the "ego mind", are only ideas, concepts, impressions, views, opinions, all arising and being birthed from the belief that we are not enough. The moment we leave this ***Central Law***, a space arises from us and the One-ness that exists. But it always rises from "I am not enough". This "I am not enough" syndrome is the cause of why we continue to search outside for more than what this planet offers us, more than what this life offers us, and therefore prevents us from experiencing life and all its beauty. Soon the pineapple, pear, orange, gets replaced with something more synthesized. 3G becomes 4G, 4G becomes 5G, 5G becomes 6G or 7G, or my house turns into the bigger house, the car that works perfectly also gets replaced, and soon the disease streams into every avenue of existence. Maybe now you will understand the Central Law, that ALL is enough, and never again will you leave your home in search for more.

Lesson

Understand the Central Law of ***Enough-ness***.

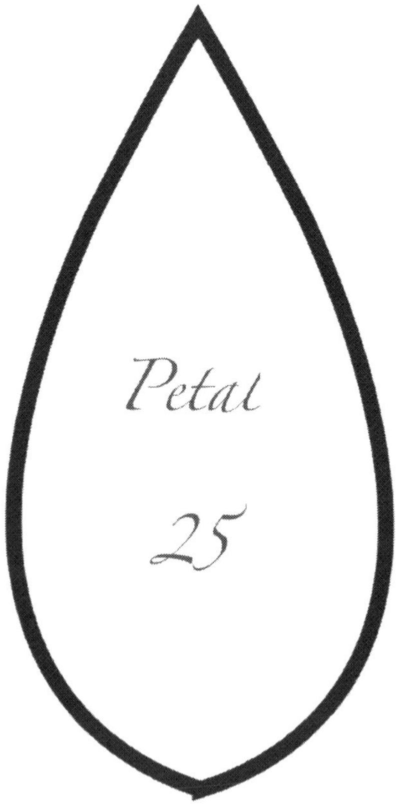
Petal
25

Petal 25

Why not cling, hold on to or grab energy? All energy, if it remains held on to, in due time will change and transform into something else. This is the ***Law of Change***. Disappointment can turn to bitterness, bitterness can turn to anger, anger can turn into revenge, and revenge can turn into hatred and so forth. But if at the moment of experiencing disappointment you are non-grabbing, non-holding, non-clinching, then the thought and emotion of disappointment will come and it will pass. A great example of this is to observe the passing clouds. Observe how they come and change their form, moving and then eventually disappearing. This is the true meaning of travelling light carrying no baggage.

Lesson

Understand that energy changes.

Petal
26

Petal 26

You are the light you seek. You are the life you want to live. You are the joy you want to experience. You are the peace you want to feel. You are the adventure you want to have. You are the gift you want to receive. You are the magic that's in the air. You are the presence you want to enjoy. You are the life in this world. The All that you see and the All that you want to experience is your ***true essence***, whispering the magical potential that you have to offer life and others. For that which is inward and that which you see is who you really are. You are ALL those things. The question is, are you courageous enough to allow them to move freely? Or will you allow the toxicity of fear to constrict your flow?

Lesson

Don't be afraid to experience the fullness of life.

Petal
27

Petal 27

Forcing, pushing, trying and striving, when life is happening by itself: your heart beating, your eyes seeing, your mind thinking, it's all happening beautifully without you. So, who is it that is trying? Who is it that is pushing? Who is it that is trying to force the moment when, in fact, the moment is just happening as it should. Have you ever considered who is the "I" that is trying? Or who is the "I" that is pushing? Awareness responds to the moment with full clarity of what is required. Very much a like a hungry child that needs feeding, it becomes one with the hunger and lets out a sound. But this is unlike someone who 'thinks' they need to eat, out of habit or comfort, and therefore putting their digestion through something that is not required. This is the difference between ***true awareness happening*** and the thinking mind. Thoughts react, awareness responds.

Lesson

We are called to respond, not react.

Petal
28

Petal 28

When the soil is dry we give it water and the water, nourishes the soil so that the seed can fall, and the plant grow. When the plant grows, the birds build their nest, and when the birds nest we hear new songs. All life gives birth to life, melody and harmony. This is the key in knowing what your true Self wants to manifest daily. It is no different to the soil, or to the water, or the plant that grows, or to the bird that nests, or to the song that's pleasant to the ear - All is part of the ***One Life***, expressing itself in different manifestations. Our joy can be seen as the soil, our compassion as the water, our giving as the plant, our comfort as the nest, our speech as the song. This is the true meaning of the Law of Life.

Lesson

All expressions of life points to your true nature.

Petal
29

Petal 29

This thing or that thing, labels and objects, names and titles are merely thoughts of what we think these objects are. But have we ever really considered what a tree might be? Or what the sun might be? Understand that the names we give people, or the titles we give them, determine how we see them, what we give them and what we receive from them. If however, we enter into life knowing that it is all a ***cosmic liquid expression*** of Universal Love, Light and Life, our receiving and our giving and our overall experience will be as it should. Therefore, be aware of the names that you give to everything and "who" is it that is giving these names? What if the air that we breathe is a secret essence or is sacred and not just air? What if the food you eat is a Love letter to every cell in your body?

Lesson

Be aware of what you name things as it determines how you treat them.

Petal
30

Petal 30

Approaching each and every 24 hour cycle with the awareness that it contains all that you require to live to its fullest is essential in you. Remain and abide in the Here and Now. For when we seek to experience life outside of our cycles we are interfering with the natural law and order of the exact rhythms that we need, and not necessarily what we want. For that which we need is essential for the "Our", and that which we want is desire for the "I". Whichever one you feed will bring its own unique experience, but understand that one feeds the All and the other feeds the "I". The truth is, the "***OUR***" is your true essence and the "I" is merely a construct, a distortion, a thought, a desire, a sensation, a feeling, an attachment, a habit.

Lesson

Be mindful of the "OUR" and not the "I" in your every day 24-hour cycle.

Petal
31

Petal 31

There is a true knowing which is based on this three-fold cord: to know is to understand, and to understand is to experience. The three working together bring the full experience of ***TRUE KNOWING***. Then there is the "I" who thinks that simply by gathering information he has truly learnt and discovered the lesson. But, in fact, it is incomplete. Nowadays with so much information available and so much information overload, the load is preventing people from truly understanding, digesting and walking through the experience. But further than this, is the allowing of your 24-hour cycle to pass through you in complete awareness. And when insight is revealed you are to act without hesitation. This is the true meaning of KNOWING something. For you can only give what you have truly passed through, then that which you give is authentic and true, living and active.

Lesson

To truly know something is to have knowledge, understanding and experience.

Petal
32

Petal 32

If you are truly awake you will soon realize that the "You" that is awake and occurring is living and experiencing without any effort. For no effort of yours is ever required in being. Your being is being without you trying. It is all happening without you. Therefore, by understanding that no effort is required one liberates oneself from the claws of tension. For zero effort, or ***effortlessness***, is the absence of the "I" and the entrance into the "Our". You are truly not required.

Lesson

No effort is required to Being.

Petal
33

Petal 33

The Universal Laws that ***co-exist*** with us are neither good nor bad and are not dependent on belief or non-belief. The Law of Space gives room. The Law of Cycles gives us time, experience and change. The Law of Cause and Effect gives all causality beginnings. All are moving together in the Here and the Now, supporting and sustaining this, moment by moment. But they are also you. And you are also them. It has been said that the Law is written in our hearts. And in fact, it is who we truly are – it is inseparable.

Lesson

We co-exist with Universal Laws.

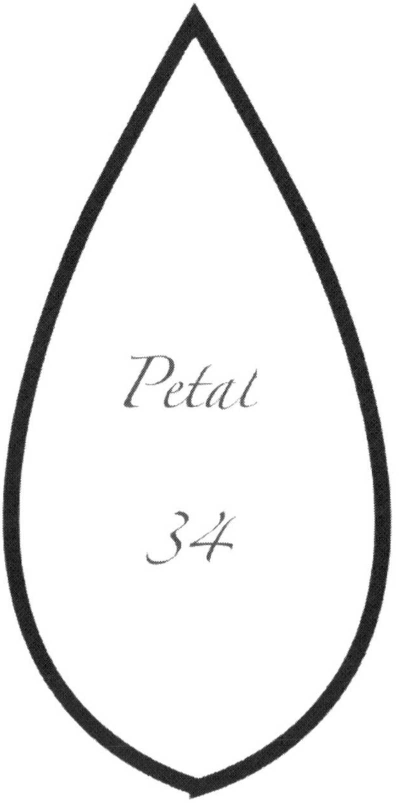
Petal
34

Petal 34

Being afraid of your fears will only paralyze you in the moment of your victory, in the moment of your liberty, in the moment where one has a grand opportunity to pass through the gateway of the past. Your fears are internal signposts and pointers, indicators of where you should be walking. So please understand that being afraid of your fears is only in the 'thought' dimension, creating a possible scenario of what you think might or could happen. The truth is, if you are in the fear of your fears, then you are more likely to be in the sensation of your fear, and therefore ***reality becomes distorted***. Your fears are opportunities for you to be liberated. Embrace them, accept them but pass through them. Become one with them. They are your guide and your teachers. They will teach you about yourself, but don't succumb to them.

Lesson

Embrace your fears as opportunities, not enemies.

Petal
35

Petal 35

With no thinking, with no mind, the Monarch butterfly reaches its destiny without a compass or a navigational system. It merely senses and becomes one with the moment of its destiny. And in joining with the moment, becoming one with the action, it accomplishes that which it sets out to do. This is the great meaning of ***sensing, knowing*** and ***acting upon***, without any hesitation. For that which is, will speak, and when it does, spread your wings and trust. For what started a work in you is faithful to complete it.

Lesson

Trust, let go and spread your wings knowing your internal compass will lead you to where you need to go.

Petal
36

Petal 36

So to know the way, the journey, the path, one does not need modern technology, navigational systems or apps, they simply need to know thyself. For to know thyself is to let go of the one that is interfering, the one that doubts, the one that thinks it knows, the one that holds on, the one that holds back, the one that separates all things, the one that is quick to judge, the one that fears or is too shy or too afraid. The letting go is trusting that which you already are, and with ***ZERO interference*** allowing the outcome to come as it is. This is the true meaning of trusting.

Lesson

Knowing thyself will lead you home.

Petal
37

Petal 37

To blame is to shame and to shame is to point the finger with distorted views. However, seeing with the eyes of your true light and true understanding is to know that we all get lost sometimes, we all miss the mark, we all become blind when we grip and hold, interfere and control. So to truly love and have compassion is to understand that on this journey we call "life", we all suffer from ignorance. Therefore, see with ***eyes to see***. See with eyes that reflect with no judgments, with no condemnation, with no shame, but reminding them of our true home. This is the meaning of looking at your brother or sister as a mirror, and when they see you they should feel and see their true abode, and know they have been homeless.

Lesson

See with your true eyes and your true essence.

Petal
38

Petal 38

To be "pure" is not a religious expression or something you need to become but rather it is what you are. For your authentic, ***true Self*** is a force that is untarnished and incorruptible, and is the true light, life and energy of the All. So it is not a question of becoming something else other than what you already are, but instead, allow your true essence the space to manifest what it already is. This is true respect of one's Self and not selling yourself short. This is allowing your true power to manifest, your true essence to live, your true light to shine. And this is what you were created for, to be WHO YOU ARE.

Lesson

Don't sell yourself short.

Petal
39

Petal 39

You may say “I live”, but do you really live? You may say “I experience life”, but which “I” is experiencing the life you are experiencing? There are two possibilities: a life in the ***“OUR”*** where all things point to the ONE - All things are working together, sustaining and supporting life. The other possibility is living life in the “I”, the “me, myself”, where your whole entire existence is pointing and supporting the “you”. Both are possibilities but let me remind you that the “me, myself and I” will never be able to experience the enough-ness of the moment. It will continue to leave the moment in search of filling the vacuum with a never-ending, quenching desire for more.

Lesson

You always have a choice.

Petal
40

Petal 40

Now, "I Am" and "I Am" is Now. I Am is Here, and Here is the I Am. If you understand the meaning of this you will understand the meaning of that which is enough, that which is whole, that which is complete, that which is full, that which is whole-hearted, that which is total, that which is ever-present, that which is your true nature, that which is you true light, that which is your true source and that which is living without you. "I am this and this, is I am". It is all ONE. Remain always with this in mind and give no space for the "I" to leave the "Am" or the "Am" to leave the "I" – this the meaning of the zero (0) and the one (1), and the 1 and the 0.

1 0

0 1

Lesson

Know the 1 and the 0, and the zero and the one.

Printed in Great Britain
by Amazon

46073539R00052